Contents

The
Sculpture
of
GRAINGER McKOY

Introduction by Robin R. Salmon
Essay by James Kilgo

WYRICK & COMPANY

BROWN PELICANS
1994, Black walnut and metal
The Sanderling Inn

Foreword

Brookgreen Gardens was the nation's first sculpture garden. Since 1931 it has quietly been building the country's most impressive collection of American figurative sculpture and has been displaying that collection in its outdoor settings. Today the Brookgreen collection includes over 700 works and provides a virtually comprehensive exhibition of sculpture created by American artists working in the naturalistic style.

Brookgreen, however, has never collected works in wood, focusing instead on sculptures of stone and metal. The reason for the exclusion of wooden pieces is obvious—such works could not endure in Brookgreen's outdoor exhibits. This is an unfortunate limitation because the earliest American sculptors worked in wood, carving figures for the bows of ships and for other ornamental uses. While the mainstream of American figurative sculpture moved on to works of stone and then of metal, some artists have continued to work with wood. Within that tradition animals, particularly birds, have served as subjects. The result of this work ranges from strictly utilitarian objects such as the crudest hunting decoys, to carvings that are almost documentary in their attempt to replicate the details of a species, to occasionally (indeed, very occasionally) work of intricate detail that also reflects an imagination and power that clearly lifts it to the level of art.

Happily, Brookgreen Gardens recently opened the Callie and John Rainey Sculpture Pavilion containing galleries that allow for the indoor exhibition of sculpture, including wooden sculpture. And happily, Grainger McKoy, one of our South Carolina neighbors, creates such sculpture (and, as you will see, bronzes now as well) at the highest level of artistic accomplishment. Thus this exhibit, "The Sculpture of Grainger McKoy," marks an important milestone in Brookgreen's long commitment to American figurative sculpture and provides for those who will see it what we are confident will be a compelling experience.

Our appreciation goes to Grainger McKoy for his artistic gifts and for his many contributions to the creation of this exhibition, to the owners of Grainger's works who graciously made them available to us, and to Robin Salmon, Brookgreen's Curator of Sculpture, who produced the exhibition.

LAWRENCE HENRY
President and Chief Executive Officer
Brookgreen Gardens

SANDERLINGS
1986 Basswood, walnut, metal, and oil paint
Collection of Earl F. Slick

Introduction

When Brookgreen Gardens was founded in 1931, Archer Huntington wrote a statement that eloquently expressed his intent and the future direction for the first public sculpture garden in America. He began with these beautiful words: "Brookgreen Gardens is a quiet joining of hands between science and art...."[1] Through the years, Brookgreen Gardens has grown and developed into a cultural entity having no peer. There are parallels that can be drawn and comparisons that can be made with other outdoor sculpture museums, but there are no others that are based on Archer Huntington's unique formula. It is this joining of science and art and, in particular, its end product, that is presented in "The Sculpture of Grainger McKoy."

Take one look at a composition by Grainger McKoy and, if you know anything about his art, you will instantly recognize it as his work. The unmistakable gravity-defying complexity of his compositions and the faithfulness to realism in the depiction are sure signs of a work by Grainger McKoy. An additional key is a meticulously deft touch that stems from the confidence of an artist who knows his subject from years of observation and experience.

Grainger McKoy's work stands alone in the recent history of American art. It is extremely difficult to find artists who create sculpture comparable in every respect with his work. Others have applied the same methods to the identical subject matter, but there are none who have achieved the same results. To be sure, there are eminent sculptors today who specialize in figures of birds. The elegant bronzes of Elliot Offner, Sandy Scott, Leo Osborne, and Kent Ullberg immediately come to mind, as well as the delicately perfect renderings by Eugene Morelli. Osborne and Morelli also work in wood; however, Osborne's woodcarvings rely on the strength of the material, often leaving untouched a portion of the wood block. Moreover, he has experimented with the application of dye on the carved areas to achieve more natural colors. Morelli has taken his work a step further by actually painting both his wood and bronze creations.

Grainger McKoy recreates the bird and its habitat with startlingly lifelike realism. There is no subterfuge; no key is necessary to interpret the action. All that is required is a cursory familiarity with the bird and its habits—and even that knowledge is not absolutely necessary. This does not mean that a McKoy sculpture is simplistic. On the contrary, it can be richly symbolic and filled with details that only the most astute naturalist will recognize. Its composition can be so complicated that it defies belief as well as gravity. The viewer walks away wondering "Could this really happen?" The answer is an emphatic "Yes!" Every activity presented in a sculpture by Grainger McKoy is based on vast knowledge of the bird and its habits coupled with dedication to accuracy in its depiction.

What has placed Grainger McKoy in his niche of prominence? First, we can examine the work of McKoy's mentor, Gilbert Maggioni, a painter, sculptor, and avid outdoorsman who made a living operating a family-owned oyster cannery in Beaufort, South Carolina. According to essayist James Kilgo, Maggioni was not the first artist to insert carved feathers into a basswood body and thereby create a more life-like bird.[2] But the manner in which he did it—a *trompe l'oeil* ("fool the eye") of the highest quality—sets his work apart from the rest.

It was Grainger McKoy, Maggioni's fledgling apprentice fresh out of college, who took this refinement and refined it still more. To dismiss this method as "wooden taxidermy" is to ignore the differences the method allows: these birds are not static, posed portraits—they pulse with life. Imagine walking through a grassy field. Suddenly, a flock of birds bursts in flight from the underbrush. You have flushed a covey of quail and, if the scene were videotaped, you could freeze the rapid motion and capture a split-second of the frantic action— the sense of movement, the accurate color and markings of the quail, the correct positions of wings and bodies. Perhaps, as you replay the videotape, you may recapture your initial feeling of surprise. But, even with the magic of videotape, it is difficult to re-experience that first, heart-stopping moment of the actual event.

A Grainger McKoy sculpture is like that videotape freeze-frame, with one important difference: the moment is depicted with three-dimensional clarity, and it is so lifelike that your first impulse is to reach out and touch the beautiful feathers and the warm body that you know must lie beneath those feathers.

Well-known wildlife artist Bob Kuhn has remarked that good representational painters always have a strong design aspect in their work. Some use very simple, basic shapes, but the excitement of their work comes from the surface treatment and the use of color. An artist's ability to take the viewer into the very midst of nature, almost into the minds of the animals, is what makes him a good wildlife artist.[3] Grainger McKoy has that ability. When we look at his sculpture of a covey rising from the ground, we feel the wings beat around us—indeed, we feel the very spontaneity of the moment.

A brief examination of the roots of wildlife art in

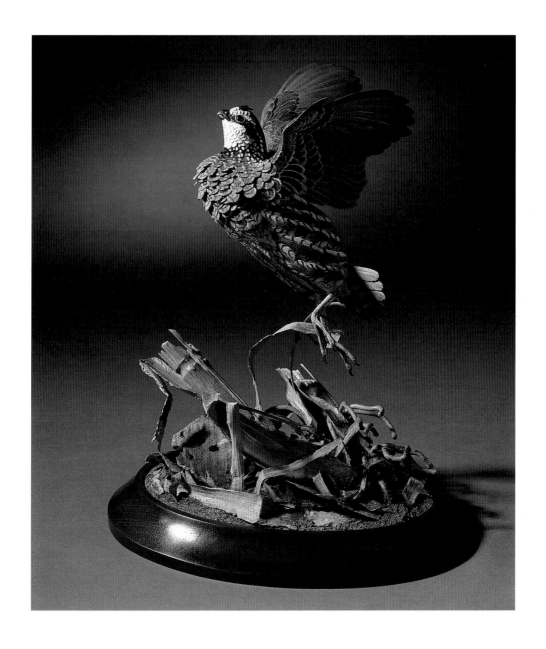

QUAIL RISING
1983 Basswood, metal, and oil paint
Collection of Marshall Field V

America will give us the historical perspective to better understand the work of Grainger McKoy. Setting aside the body of artistic work by Native Americans, the first wildlife artists on this continent were European naturalists who strove for accurate, true-to-nature depictions of their subjects. These explorers found a wilderness of forests, swamps, and rivers, particularly in the South, where the combination of sun, rain, and fertile soil created a place of abundant vegetation and wildlife. The explorers made botanical and zoological drawings to record as precisely as possible the new sights for royal patrons and other financial backers. Complete landscapes were sketched to present the scope of animal habitats. This adherence to realism has always been important in the artwork of Southern artists. "Southerners," observes Lisa Howorth of the Center for the Study of Southern Culture at the University of Mississippi, "value above all their ties with the natural world. This connection to the natural world is one of the first threads to find expression in Southern art and literature. The South was, without a doubt, a paradise for European naturalists, whose accounts of the New World...express a stunned sensibility, an overload of stimuli ranging from interaction with exotic native people—the first Southerners—and the luxuriant vegetation, to examination of fantastic and unknown forms of animal life."[4]

John Lawson (before 1675-1711) was one of the earliest of the explorer-naturalists. He traveled throughout the Southeast several times and eventually died in North Carolina after he was captured by members of the Tuscarora tribe. His controlled drawings of native species are often surprisingly accurate, especially when they are compared to the works of his contemporaries. One of the first South Carolina artists was John Drayton

WREN ON LOCK
1996, Bronze

(1710-1779), for whom the classically inspired Drayton Hall on the Ashley River near Charleston was built. He produced amazingly good pencil sketches of native birds finished with watercolors, some of which survive today. His interest in the plants and animals around him stemmed from a passion for hunting and fishing, a circumstance noted by more than one scholar of Southern history and art.[5] During the same period, Mark Catesby (1682-1749) was collecting and painting birds along the Ashley River for his *Natural History of Carolina, Georgia, Florida and the Bahama Islands*, the first extensive published portrayal of the region's flora and fauna.

John James Audubon (1785-1851) was among the first to turn his talents in a direction that elevated the scientific renderings of the naturalists to a level of fine art. Like other early wildlife artists, he collected his own specimens and often moved to locations in order to be closer to his subjects. Largely self-taught, Audubon was devoted to illustrating the birds of North America at life-size in "lively attitudes" and in native habitats. He shot most of his own specimens, wired them upright, and made quick pencil sketches that were transferred to drawing paper. Later, these more detailed drawings were enhanced with pastels and watercolors. Audubon concentrated on the birds; his assistants, including his wife

and sons, painted the backgrounds. These watercolor backgrounds, which sometimes included the distant skylines of cities such as Charleston and Key West or landmark Southern lighthouses, added an extra measure of realism to the two-dimensional compositions.

Because so many Southerners in the nineteenth century loved the outdoors and its many recreational opportunities, there was a steady market for paintings of game to hang over dining room sideboards and portraits of champion thoroughbred horses to display in offices and

WOOD ORIGINAL FOR WILD TURKEYS (TWO TOMS)
1996

SPARROW HAWK
1998, Bronze

other male domains. Today, this passion continues to inspire artists and to produce collectors of their art. In the twentieth century, yet another element of artistic inspiration has been introduced: the desire to record the flora and fauna of a given region before it becomes extinct. As habitats disappear and numbers of native species dwindle, a new kind of artist, one concerned with the environment, has emerged. The goal of the environmental artist—like that of his seventeenth- and eighteenth-century counterpart, the explorer-naturalist—is to depict accurately the natural world.

Given this historical background, it is not surprising that Grainger McKoy's work is sought avidly by both collectors and museums. He has bridged the gap between anatomical accuracy and fine art in a manner that sets his work apart from other practitioners in the field of sculpture. The late nineteenth-century painters of *nature morte* specialized in portraying obviously dead specimens of game dangling upside down by a string suspended from a nail driven into a rough board—the ultimate *trompe l'oeil*. The very antithesis of *nature morte*, McKoy's works are full of life.

Since 1995, he has added a new dimension to his body of work. Just as he successfully launched groups of carved birds into airy, yet convincing compositions, he now presents the same feeling of flight in bronze castings of his avian subjects. By taking molds directly from his woodcarvings and using a vacuum-casting method, McKoy is exploring a new artistic direction. The use of bronze has brought with it a challenge to stretch the capabilities of the medium. The very form of a bronze bird now emphasizes movement and line. Individual striations and color patterns of feathers have emerged in the bronze, eliminating the need for elaborate patination to achieve beautiful detail. Glass has been added to the eye sockets of some birds, providing a historic link with the use of enamel, precious metal, and polished stone as accents in the sculpture of ancient Egypt, the Middle East, and Asia.

This marks not only a major change in Grainger McKoy's work, but the beginning of his effort to push bronze to new limits. To be sure, movement and line continue to be important elements in his carved sculpture. It is clear that he does not see the use of metal as a

SPARROW HAWK
Detail

boundary or limitation. On the contrary, with each design he tests the metal as he tested the wood, and he nurtures the growth of his wood sculpture in response to its role as a model for bronze. Now, the pure linear qualities of the design come to the fore as McKoy explores and perfects the possibilities of metal. His growth as an artist—no less faithful to realism, but challenging in the transition from carved and painted wood to cast and subtly patinated bronze—is presented in this exhibition.

"The Sculpture of Grainger McKoy" is a landmark exhibition in two separate arenas: Brookgreen Gardens as a museum and Grainger McKoy as a sculptor. Many of the innovative bronzes in this exhibition are on public view for the first time. Indeed, some were created specifically for the exhibition. Likewise, through the generosity of individual owners, many of the extraordinary wood sculptures are being shown in South Carolina for the first time in this exhibition. Finally,

"The Sculpture of Grainger McKoy" is the first temporary indoor exhibition at Brookgreen Gardens of artworks from beyond its own sculpture collection.

In 1931, Archer Huntington closed his inaugural statement on the founding of Brookgreen Gardens with this counsel: "In all due homage to science it may be well not to forget inspiration, the sister of religion, without whose union this world might yet become a desert."[6] After viewing a sculpture by Grainger McKoy, it is easy to discern the genius of the artwork. What is not so apparent is the genius of the artist. Infused with warmth, sincerity, and a humility that somehow seems at odds with its source, this genius is perplexing at first. But once the viewer learns that in Grainger McKoy's world everything springs from a spiritual source, it begins to make sense. After all, as Archer Huntington prophetically concluded so many years ago, spirituality and creativity go hand in hand.

ROBIN R. SALMON
Vice President and Curator of Sculpture
Brookgreen Gardens

NOTES

1. *Brookgreen Gardens History* (Murrells Inlet, S.C.: Brookgreen Gardens, 1954), p. 6.

2. James Kilgo, *Bird Sculpture in Wood by Grainger McKoy*, exh. cat. (Chadds Ford, PA.: Brandywine River Museum, 1993), p. 16.

3. Tom Davis, *The Art of Bob Kuhn*, as quoted in *Wildlife: The Artist's View*, exh. cat. (Wausau, Wis.: Leigh Yawkey Woodson Art Museum, 1990), pgs. 8 & 12.

4. Lisa Howorth, ed., *The South: A Treasury of Art and Literature* (Oxford, Miss.: Hugh Lauter Levin Associates, Inc., 1993), p. 12.

5. Howorth, *The South: A Treasury of Art and Literature*, p. 15; Randolph Delehanty, *Art in the American South: Works from the Ogden Collection* (Baton Rouge, LA and London: Louisiana State University Press, 1996), p. 8.

6. *Brookgreen Gardens History*, p. 8.

*"This sculpture came into focus when I read in Exodus about
God's sending quail into the camp of the Israelites, and I supposed
Moses must have been the first to reach for supper."*

AMERICAN WOODCOCK
1996, Bronze

Acknowledgements

There are many people who make a project of this scope and significance possible. Some of them do it as a part of their daily work, performing with excellence as the goal. Others do it as a gift to those who participate in the project, providing encouragement, suggestions, and stepping stones toward the success and quality of the exhibition.

First, the extraordinary vision and talent of Grainger McKoy provided the impetus for this project. His overall contribution to the exhibition is immeasurable. I thank him for his diligence and patience during the two-year planning and implementation period. I am grateful for his expertise in transporting and installing works in the exhibition—a most significant task. His wife, Floride, provided the warmth and insight necessary to build a foundation for an artist's creativity and then to allow it to grow. Her graciousness has made this project a pleasure.

Kay Teer, working on behalf of Grainger McKoy, brings to her duties a deep-seated determination and ability tempered by an elegance that could serve as a model for other women in the business world. The technical expertise of Ed Fenton deserves recognition, as he makes it possible to translate Grainger McKoy's wooden creations into bronze. His understanding of the medium's requirements is in complete accord with the sculptor's goals.

A special group made possible the catalogue and their contributions resulted in a distinctive publication. They are: Mel Schockner of Loveland, Colorado, and Ted Borg of Chapin, South Carolina, two of the best photographers of sculpture in America; James Kilgo, Professor of English, the University of Georgia, whose definitive essay on Grainger McKoy's work from the Brandywine River Museum in 1993 was revised and expanded in this publication; Gil Shuler of Gil Shuler Graphic Design, Inc. in Charleston, South Carolina, who was responsible for the catalogue's beautiful design; and Wyrick & Company in Charleston, who edited and published the catalogue.

I am indebted to Doyle Cotton, Marshall Field V, William R. Ireland, John A. Luetkemeyer, Jr., Dan W. Lufkin, Richard P. Mellon, John M. Rivers, Jr., Earl F. Slick, and Anne D. Wolff who recognize Grainger McKoy's unique talents and are willing to share these talents with others by lending works to this exhibition.

Finally, thanks are reserved for the Brookgreen Gardens Board of Trustees, who had the courage to approve this first exhibition of sculpture outside the institution's collection.

ROBIN R. SALMON
Vice President and Curator of Sculpture

Artist's Acknowledgements

While preparing for this exhibit and tracing my trail of sawdust to Brookgreen, I realized again that none of these birds could have arrived alone. My mother, who yielded a log corner of our cabin for my first bird, my older brothers, Adair and Pete, who cheered my every attempt, and Gilbert Maggioni, who challenged me as no one had before, were my earliest supporters.

Friends with whom I've spent many hours afield and about the hearth sharing experiences and faith—Carlton Fraylick, Jim Kilgo, Robert Marshall, Jim Meunier, Johnnie Corbett, Carlyle Blakeney, Rick Belser, Micah LaRoche, Rowland Alston, Polk Sanders, Johnny Mikell, Alan Wooten, Bruce Jackson, Meredith Drakeford, and John Barr, to name a few—have in many ways sculpted these birds as much as I have.

A special thanks to all my patrons, of whom only a few have works in this exhibit. Most especially I am grateful to Mr. and Mrs. Earl F. Slick, who began collecting my visions 25 years ago, many of which are exhibited at the Sanderling Inn, Duck, North Carolina. I deeply appreciate the confidence they have shown in me throughout this journey.

Without the dedication and focus of Kay Teer, Robin Salmon, and Ed Fenton and all the unique gifts that they brought with them, this exhibition would not have been possible.

I have been both humbled and stimulated by the opportunity Lawrence Henry and the Brookgreen Board have given me to be the first sculptor to exhibit from outside their collection. To them and to all the Brookgreen staff I extend my thanks.

For my children, Grainger, Beth, and Mary Adair, and especially my wife Floride, who has been my greatest source of encouragement next to God, I give thanks. To them and to those mentioned above I dedicate this catalogue.

PRELIMINARY SKETCH FOR COVEY RISE

He will cover you with his wings; you will be safe in his care;
his faithfulness will protect and defend you.
PSALM 91:4

Whatever your hand finds to do, do it with your might.
Ecclesiastes 9:10

The Art of Grainger McKoy

When in 1969 a new acquaintance of mine insisted that I drive down to his home in Savannah, Georgia, to see a couple of carvings made by a friend of his, I thought the trip a waste of time. Though I was enthusiastic about bird art, I had little interest in painted wooden ducks.

"He does carve ducks," the man said, "but these are shorebirds, an oystercatcher and a willet. You wouldn't believe how good."

He was right. Nothing I had ever seen or heard prepared me for the oystercatcher. This was no static portrait piece but a desperate moment in the life of the bird, its scarlet blade of a beak imprisoned by a clamped oyster, its wings backstroking frantically in its effort to free itself. The bird was carved life size, and its plumage glowed with a feathery sheen I would not have thought possible from paint on wood.

"Count the primaries," my host said.

The number was correct.

"Do you reckon that ever happened?" I asked. "I mean an oystercatcher caught by an oyster?"

"It's possible. Gilbert's a good naturalist."

"Gilbert" was Gilbert Maggioni, owner and operator of an oyster-packing factory in nearby Beaufort, South Carolina, a saltwater man, my host explained. The other carving was quieter—a willet preening a down feather from the elbow of a slightly opened wing.

"Notice the snail?" asked my host.

There was a bulge in the bird's throat the size of a marble.

"That's a big part of the willet's diet."

What I felt most strongly that afternoon was not a longing to own these pieces but a desire to carve such birds myself. The paintings of Louis Agassiz Fuertes and George Miksch Sutton had lately rekindled my passion for birds, first awakened by John James Audubon's images when I was a child. For the past two years I had been drawing from live models in the field and from roadkills in the studio. Now Maggioni's carving presented the possibility of a more exciting medium. I wanted to meet him.

"I don't think so," said my host. "Gilbert's not what you'd call a gregarious fellow. I wouldn't want to impose on our friendship."

I imagined a crusty old hermit, far out on the marsh, whittling away with oyster-scarred hands.

"Besides, he's already got an apprentice, a Clemson student named Grainger McKoy."

What I felt then was envy. If Grainger McKoy was a college student he must be at least five years younger than I, and he was already well on his way toward achieving the success that I was only dreaming of.

rainger McKoy was born in 1947, youngest son of a couple who by grace and good sense set an example to their children of independence and integrity. Adair and Priscilla McKoy were cousins to each other, grandchildren of a socially prominent Wilmington, North Carolina, banker and his wife. Feeling unsuited for the society life to which they were born, they moved in the early years of their marriage with their three boys to Sumter, South Carolina, where Adair took a position as manager of a mill supply store. When Grainger was five, his parents moved into a primitive rural cabin of cypress they had built themselves. "Back to the earth," McKoy has said, "at least ten years before that kind of thing became popular."

Almost immediately Adair began to educate his sons in the ways of rural life. To teach them the difference between poisonous and nonpoisonous snakes, he put two barrels in the yard, one for each kind, to be collected alive. When young Adair, who now owns and operates a large tomato farm on Wadmalaw Island, South Carolina, expressed interest in planting a crop, his father went into debt to buy him a tractor. For Peter, who was to become a veterinarian, he drove down to Daytona, Florida, to pick up a horse that a friend had offered the boy. He would surely have provided similar

encouragement to his youngest son, but when Grainger was nine Adair McKoy died of a heart attack.

The sudden loss was devastating to the entire family, but Priscilla did her best to continue her husband's encouragement of their sons' interests. One of Grainger's strongest childhood memories is of his mother holding him up by the back of his trousers so that he could saw off the end of a cypress log that was part of the cabin. He wanted to carve a bird and the end of that log was the best available wood, so his mother, placing more importance on her son's creative impulse than on the appearance of the house, had said, "Let's do it." On Saturdays she drove him to Columbia seventy miles round trip, for drawing lessons at The Columbia Museum of Art. Once she took him to the Library of Congress, where they looked up titles on ducks and decoys. There McKoy became acquainted with Frank Kortright's *Ducks, Geese, and Swans of North America* and Edgar Queeny's *Prairie Wings*—books that were destined to play a critical role in his development.

Like most boys of his generation, McKoy played high school sports and went out with girls, but his passion was birds—game birds and hunting. When his grandmother sent him an antique decoy for Christmas, the gift inspired him to carve his own. Synthetics were

Grainger with his children in 1974 at his first studio on Wadmalaw Island, SC.

available, lightweight and inexpensive, but he preferred wood, and he wanted to hunt ducks using decoys he had carved himself. When he fell in love with Floride Owens, whom he had known since the third grade, the best present he could think to give her was a shorebird he had whittled out of cypress.

These early efforts caught the eye of a man who knew quality when he saw it; he suggested that McKoy show his work to a friend of his in Beaufort. The friend was Gilbert Maggioni. Recognizing immediately McKoy's skill, he invited the boy to come down and work with him. In spite of the difference in their ages—Maggioni was old enough to be McKoy's father—their mutual passion for wildlife and art developed into friendship. When McKoy was a sophomore at Clemson, studying architecture, he and brother Adair took Maggioni to hunt geese at their grandparents' farm in Maryland. An Episcopal church in nearby Chestertown was sponsoring a show of decoys and decorative bird carving that weekend and the goose hunters paused to take it in.

The purpose of the duck decoy of course is to fool wary ducks into approaching the hunter's blind. To accomplish that, the decoy must resemble the species being hunted. How closely is a matter of dispute, but hunters agree that fine brushwork is wasted as far as the duck is concerned. Much of a decoy's charm derives from its simplified colors and plumage patterns. When by the early sixties, synthetics made decoys carved from the heavier wooden blocks obsolete, such men as Steve and Lem Ward of Crisfield, Maryland, turned to producing "mantelpiece birds," which could be finished in much greater detail than those required for hunting, and realism quickly became an end in itself. It was just a matter of time before nongame species—especially owls and songbirds—began to appear at shows and competitions. By today's standards these early efforts, designated "decorative," were crude and simple: birds stuck at unnatural

SHORE BIRD
Carved by Grainger in 1960

angles onto pieces of driftwood. According to a story that has been repeated many times, Maggioni said something like, "Hell, Grainger, we could do better than that." What is less widely known is the significance of that moment to McKoy: for the first time he felt that Maggioni accepted him as a peer. "We?" McKoy thought, exhilarated. It was a turning point.

Two years later, at the Second Annual Atlantic Flyway Wildfowl Carving and Arts Exhibit at Salisbury, Maryland, Maggioni uncrated a life-size wild turkey, *in flight*, its primaries and tail feathers individually carved and inserted. No one had ever seen anything like it. Yet the carving provoked as much consternation as applause. Some disgruntled competitors dismissed it as wooden taxidermy, and the wife of one carver, not entirely joking, said to Maggioni, "We hate you." Whether or not they really did, they certainly began to imitate his work. In the next year or two carved birds with inserted feathers began appearing at the shows.

Gilbert Maggioni was not the first carver to insert wooden feathers nor was he the first to use a soldering iron to burn in feather detail, but he and McKoy, who was spending summers working in the shop, so refined those techniques that they achieved an unprecedented degree of realism. It was almost impossible to look at

GILBERT MAGGIONI
Beaufort, South Carolina

"Gilbert was the first real artist I'd ever met. He challenged me like no one had before or since. He kept his foot on my neck and held me accountable to the bird."

their birds without wanting to touch them, to confirm with one's fingers the illusion of soft plumage.

By the time McKoy graduated from Clemson (having changed his major from architecture to zoology) Maggioni knew that his gifted protégé had the ability to become a successful bird artist. He wanted the young man to commit himself to full-time carving, but McKoy had married his sweetheart Floride, and Grainger Jr. had arrived. Maggioni's proposal involved a great risk. "Try it for six months," the older man persisted. "Move down here and see. If it doesn't work out, at least you can say you tried."

McKoy spent an eighteen-month apprenticeship in Maggioni's shop, a grueling schedule with long hours set by a man who had no family to go home to. Yet McKoy looks back on that time as one of the most exciting periods of his life. Stimulated by each other's passion for innovation and experimentation, the two carvers grew increasingly ingenious in their use of inserts, more and more adept at simulating plumage, and ever bolder in suspending and supporting birds in flight. Firing each other's imagination, they singlehandedly transformed bird carving from craft to art.

Maggioni modestly disclaims credit as McKoy's mentor: they were partners who worked together on equal terms, challenging each other and sharing discoveries but pursuing separate courses. But McKoy insists that he learned much from Maggioni in technique and more importantly a faith in the artistic possibilities of his work. "Gilbert made an artist of me," McKoy says. At Maggioni's suggestion they visited the great art museums in Washington and New York. Maggioni introduced McKoy to the watercolors of Winslow Homer at the National Gallery of Art and the French animal bronzes at the Metropolitan Museum of Art. The bronzes, rather than the increasingly realistic carvings that were beginning to take ribbons at national competitions, became the standard by which they measured their efforts.

It was during McKoy's apprenticeship period that I saw the oystercatcher and willet. Shortly after, McKoy moved up the coast to Wadmalaw Island, where in the front yard of his brother Adair's house he converted an abandoned country store into a workshop. He and Floride had two children, and it was time to see if he could support his family by carving birds.

Like those grand masters of the late fifteenth and early sixteenth century (Tilman Riemenschneider and Viet Stoss), McKoy enshrines a sense of the permanent with a fine, feathery touch.

Thomas Hoving

BRONZE DETAIL
OF *DEAD BIRD*

The first important showing of McKoy's work came five years later at the American Museum of Natural History, New York, in the spring of 1974. Together he and Maggioni took twenty-one pieces to New York, nine of them major sculptures, including McKoy's *Wood Ducks*, a pair of birds flaring through the branches of an autumn sweet gum; *Three Green-winged Teal*, three ducks settling onto a cattail pond; *Red-tailed Hawk and Pheasant*, the swooping raptor clutching the tail feathers of its panicked prey; *Green Herons*, three birds dancing in an oriental calligraphy, fighting for a fish; and the magnificent *Red-shouldered Hawks and Copperhead Snake*, the two frantically flapping hawks grappling in a tug-of-war for the snake, the tail of which is wrapped around a clump of broom sedge in a desperate knot that supports the sculpture. Maggioni's work was equally dramatic—birds on the wing frozen in instants of aggression, struggle, or alarm.

New York was unprepared for works like these. Arts reporters were so excited by the startlingly realistic renderings that they hardly noticed the more impressive achievement of birds being carved in flight and suspended or supported by cleverly concealed armatures.[1] Though in recent years other carvers have produced work as daringly designed as McKoy's early pieces, no one in 1974 was even attempting to use birds to support other birds in flight. Writer Roger Schroeder notes:

> It took South Carolinian Grainger McKoy to put birds together in flight. In 1972, McKoy finished a red-tailed hawk chasing a pheasant....What holds the hawk above the gamebird is a single tail feather that the red-tail clutches in one foot. With this quantum leap, there seemed to be no limit to what a steel suspension system could do.[2]

In the autumn of 1975 McKoy's *Red-shouldered Hawks and Copperhead Snake* appeared in "Animals in Art" at the Royal Ontario Museum in Toronto. Assembling work as diverse as serigraphs of prehistoric European cave painting, Inuit soapstone carving, watercolors by John James Audubon, and McKoy's realistic wood sculpture, the exhibition challenged the critical assumption that "wildlife art" is an inferior category closer to illustration than to serious art. It helped to establish McKoy as a major wildlife artist.

"This idea was triggered after observing the bold, hunger-induced behavior of an immature red-shouldered hawk blundering in upon an adult trying to make a meal of a copperhead."

oon after McKoy returned from Toronto I received a call from my sister. Her husband, an Episcopal priest, had recently moved to a church on John's Island, South Carolina, next door to Wadmalaw. "Grainger McKoy is a member of the parish," she said. He didn't attend church often, but they had met him. He was a nice guy. Why didn't I come on down? They would introduce me.

I had hacked out a working decoy or two and recently completed a decorative widgeon. I was bold enough to take the widgeon with me.

The road from Saint John's rectory out to Wadmalaw ran straight and flat through a landscape of rural poverty-run-down mobile homes scattered among moss-hung live oaks. After thirty minutes I was beginning to think that Grainger McKoy had retreated as far as possible from the beaten path; from what I had read about him, he sounded like the type. A recent article had said that he was "completely uncomfortable in the public role of 'successful artist,'" and that he might be mistaken at first for "an angry young man caught up in an ego trip that excludes the rest of the world."[3] I hoped my brother-in-law knew what he was doing.

We pulled off the blacktop in front of an old, tin-roofed country store, an abandoned enterprise used now for housing fertilizer and farm equipment, from what I could tell. In the yard around back stood a large wire cage containing six or eight green-winged teal—diminutive drakes and hens—and cats of all sizes prowled about the steps. We announced ourselves with a knock, entered, and were greeted by the whine of a band saw.

A young man stood at the machine, in a spray of fragrant sawdust, powdered khaki from head to foot. He was guiding with both hands a large block of light-colored wood, using the dangerous blade as deftly as a pocketknife. If he noticed us, he showed no sign of it, but, totally concentrated, angled the block first one way and then another, carving curved faces.

Gradually, I noticed objects—another band saw, a freezer, glass-encased bookshelves, an antique school desk, an array of chisels and gouges spread on a work bench, a sleeping yellow lab, and in one corner a floor-to-ceiling cage containing an injured red-tailed hawk that regarded us with a baleful amber eye. But it was the object in the center of the floor that gave meaning to the clutter—a sculpture of five small ducks in flight. Burned a uniform umber but not yet painted, it had the appeal of an unfinished work, the individual birds arrested at a point between the blocks of basswood out

"As a young teenager, I hung a wood duck on my porch while I ate supper. When I returned to my prize, the croker sack I had been carrying it in wasn't as strong as I had thought, and my duck was caught again—this time in the midst of an escape."

WOOD DUCK IN A CROKER SACK
1993, Basswood, tupelo and oil paint
Collection of the artist

of which they had been carved and the neat little teal they were on their way to becoming, still obviously wood but already twisting and tumbling downward against the resistance of a cold wind. More powerfully than any sporting print I had ever seen, it evoked the throat-tightening excitement that hunters feel most keenly at the sight and sounds of wild ducks coming in.

While the individual birds were positioned wingtip to wingtip, the entire squadron was supported by a wind-bent reed. To ask how Grainger had wrought that marvel seemed as crass as inquiring about the price.

I walked around to the other side, admired it from that perspective. By its form the sculpture created its own space, seemed in fact to make its own weather. I could neither take my eyes from it nor look at it for very long at a time.

The noise of the band saw ceased. Grainger wiped his hands on his khakis and turned to greet us. He stood above medium height, a solidly built young man, his hair thick and dark, and his face asserted itself in a prominent brow and chin. But the feature that predominated through the powder of sawdust was the eyes; clear and steel-gray, they shone with seriousness of purpose. He extended his hand, and I was reminded suddenly of the clunky decoy I was holding in mine.

Grainger was polite, found something to compliment. Then to my surprise he said that if I was serious about carving and had the time I was welcome to come down and work with him. "Just bring your pocketknife and sleeping bag," he said.

I took him up on the offer. In December of '75 I spent three days in his shop. He was working hard, preparing for an exhibition at Hammer Galleries on Fifty-seventh Street in New York, the most prestigious venue yet for showing his work, but he took time to rough out a green-winged teal decoy, carve one side of it, and turn it over to me. I considered my task. Grainger had replicated a swimming drake, a bird he had observed from a hunter's blind and studied in the hand; he had outlined a folded wing overlapped by tertiary and flank feathers, carved

The carvings speak for themselves, they convey controlled energy embodied in vivid detail. The result is pure, natural, and unsurpassable quality, the hallmark of a hugely creative talent.

O. Kelley Anderson, Jr., Coe Kerr Gallery

upper-wing coverts and primaries—each feather separate and distinct—and with a Fordham tool worked
in the texture of breast and back plumage. My job
was to imitate Grainger, to make my side of the
decoy as much like his as possible.

I started with the head, which required
measurements with calipers—distance
from tip of bill to base, from
base to eye, from eye to top of
head. When I had
done that, he
showed me how
to cut a cavity for
the glass taxidermy
eye (the use of which
seemed a bit impure to me despite the goal
of absolute realism), how to fit the eye through
the opening, which was oval thus smaller than the
circular glass, and how to bring the eye up into a natural position—a tricky business. Then, as smoothly as
if he were drawing with pen and ink, he burned in
feather detail on his side of the teal with a soldering-
iron knife. When he handed it back to me, the decoy
looked half-dressed, one side naked basswood, the
other a literal burnt umber glowing with a lovely

ARTIST'S STUDY

sheen that only burning can produce. It seemed a
shame to paint it. But decorative carving is a descendent of the painted wooden decoy, and the genre is
restricted by its ancestry. After burning my side, I
painted the whole duck as realistically as I could.

But to what end? To attract wary buyers? Even as
I strove to make my side of the teal indistinguishable
from Grainger's, a question nagged at the back of
my mind: what then? Not yet thirty, Grainger was
already closer to the carver's goal of absolute realism
than anyone I knew of. But once he achieved it,
what would he do with the rest of his life? Surely
there was more to carving
than impressing people
whose highest praise
was to say that they
couldn't tell his work
from taxidermy.
I had not heard then of
Walter Anderson, but I considered the birds of Audubon
and nineteenth-century
Swedish painter Bruno
Liljefors and others whose
work I had seen in the

Animals in Art catalogue. Though the subjects were portrayed realistically enough for ornithologists to identify—a weakness according to many highbrow critics—their paintings nevertheless showed strong aesthetic design. Could a corresponding balance be achieved in carving?

Before I left his shop Grainger made me a burning knife, and he sent me home to Georgia with enough basswood to last through six months of trial and error. When I returned to Wadmalaw the next summer, I brought with me a full-bodied blue-winged teal, and Grainger taught me to braze so that I might fashion the brass feet necessary to support the weight of the carving. Though he confessed reservations about revealing to me in one hour techniques that had taken him and Maggioni weeks of hard work to discover, he said that the only way he could repay the debt he owed his mentor was by helping others as Maggioni had helped him. Even so, I could see that he was too busy to be interrupted by any but the most urgent questions. The Hammer Galleries show was only a few months away, and he was putting in twelve to fourteen hours a day. No matter how early I arrived at his shop, he was already busy at the band saw or bent over a wing with the burning knife.

Lunch was a peanut butter and jelly sandwich on the back steps—a fifteen or twenty minute break—and then it was back to work for the long summer afternoon. When I commented on his self-discipline, he replied with surprise: "I can't think of anything I'd rather be doing."

Floride came by with the children after school every day to pick up the mail, but they seldom tarried. I asked Grainger how he managed to avoid the standard parental responsibilities of school plays and church picnics. "I told Floride a long time ago not to make me choose between them and my work," he replied.

Unannounced visitors were unwelcome. One day two women knocked on the front door. Suntanned and stylishly dressed, they were vacationing at nearby Kiawah Island and wanted to meet the famous artist. One had seen his work in her husband's *Field and Stream.* They hoped they weren't interrupting anything important, could they just take a peek? Without introducing themselves, they began to look around, oohing and aahing over Grainger's birds. Their husbands had chosen to play golf that morning, wouldn't they be sorry. Finally, one of them asked the inevitable question, "How much do you get for these things?"

McKoy produces bird sculptures in wood that are so true to life they can hardly be believed. Even if you care nothing for sculptures or for birds, they will leave you breathless.

Edward J. Sozanski, *The Philadelphia Inquirer Magazine*

PINTAILS
1991, Basswood, metal, and oil paint
Collection of John A. Luetkemeyer, Jr.

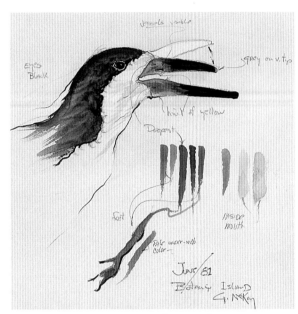

COLOR STUDY FOR BLACK SKIMMER.

Grainger said he preferred not to discuss prices unless a prospective buyer was seriously interested in making a purchase.

Oh well, she laughed, she was sure she couldn't afford anything of that quality, but her husband would kill her if she didn't find out how much. "This little bird now"—she indicated a marsh wren, the smallest carving in the shop—"what would that go for? Ballpark."

Reluctantly, Grainger mentioned a figure. The woman's mouth fell open in exaggerated disbelief. "Well," she sniffed, "I guess you do have a lot of time in it."

"We all have a lot of time in something," Grainger said.

When the women were gone, he complained that his shop was too close to civilization. "They stop in here all the time, never call ahead, and then they expect you to be grateful that they're interested in what you're doing. And all they really want is to know how much. It's like they can't appreciate a carving until they see the price tag."

Like most professional artists, Grainger sometimes felt caught in the conflict between economic necessity and artistic vision. "I could turn this shop into a duck and quail factory and make a better living," he said one day. "What I really want to carve is four or five mallards squirming out of the mouth of a croker sack. Now that would be a carving. But people would want to know what they were doing in that sack to begin with. If it's not stuck on a piece of driftwood, they don't understand it."

"But you haven't given in to that pressure," I said.

"I haven't carved that croker sack either."

That same summer, 1976, Birmingham Museum of Art held an exhibition entitled "Bird Sculpture: A Native American Art Form, Refined." The cover of the catalogue shows a pre-Paiute reed decoy, circa 1st century A.D., and in a corner inset Grainger McKoy's

His love for birds is clear, but also obvious is his acute sense of form and his constant excitement over shape and perceived movement. His eye, talent, and diligence produce his art.

James H. Duff, Director, Brandywine River Museum

Wood Ducks. The introductory essay traces the development from one to the other, pointing out that the pivotal moment occurred when the Ward brothers—Steve and Lem—began carving ornamental decoys in the 1950s.[4] That same development was reenacted by Grainger McKoy in the first twenty years or so of his life, beginning with the crude hunting blocks inspired by his grandmother's gift, and culminating at the higher level to which he and Gilbert Maggioni had recently taken decorative carving.

So conscious was I of the decoy ancestry of decorative birds that I was slow to see that Grainger's work was also a descendent of the tradition of bird portraiture established by Audubon.

Unlike Liljefors, who painted landscapes with birds (and mammals) in them, Audubon was a bird portraitist. To accomplish his goal of depicting each bird in scientifically accurate detail, he removed the subject from its natural habitat where plumage patterns conspire with sun and shadow to conceal, and placed it in the foreground, life size and artificially lighted. If that were all he had done, however, his work today would be consigned to the same dusty drawer that contains the stilted drawings made by his contemporary Alexander Wilson. Audubon, however, brought his birds to life; without

sacrificing accuracy of detail, he restored to his wired and decomposing models the raucous tilt and flashing wing that he remembered from the woods and fields, and for the first time in America, people for whom most birds had been no more than colorful blurs and wild cries could see what they really look like.

WILLET
1975, Basswood, metal, and oil paint
Collection of Dan W. Lufkin

GREEN HERONS
1973, Basswood, metal, and oil paint
Collection of Doyle Cotton

Whereas later bird artists—Liljefors and Fuertes, for example—used natural light to create form, Audubon's sensibility was governed by the neoclassical line. Delineated rather than molded, his birds reveal their distinctive colors in bright, flat patterns, and the larger, more dramatic species flash across the page in sweeping curves and bold angles. Ironically, ornithologists who want scientific illustration complain now, as they did in the nineteenth century, that Audubon's flair for romantic design distorted the subject, causing him to miss a bird's distinctive character; some art critics, on the other hand, dismiss as mere illustration paintings whose subject is wildlife accurately portrayed.

Novelist Vladimir Nabokov, recognizing the controversial nature of Audubon's images, asks, "Does there not exist a high ridge where the mountainside of 'scientific' knowledge joins the opposite slope of 'artistic' imagination?"[5] Art critic Adam Gopnik, who quotes Nabokov's question, provides an answer:

Audubon walked along [that ridge] more bracingly and with a finer equilibrium than any artist before or since. He sought facts—the exact things, peculiarities—and found them by inventing a style. In Audubon the patterning impulse and the explanatory impulse were always the same.[6]

I question Gopnik's "always," but certainly in his best work—the splendid *Pileated Woodpeckers* and *Carolina Parakeets*, for example—Audubon bridged the two with breathtaking tension.

That same tension distinguishes the major pieces McKoy presented at Hammer Galleries: *Five Green-winged Teal*, *Green Herons*, *Red-shouldered Hawks and Copperhead Snake*, and *Clapper Rails* (two birds entangled in a struggle to snatch from each other a fiddler crab that hangs suspended between their open beaks). Like Audubon, McKoy exploits in his art the extravagant possibilities inherent in the dynamics of avian form and behavior, and he does it without compromising the smallest ornithological detail. Moreover, he does it without distorting the character of the species, and he does it in wood. Undaunted by the intransigence of his chosen medium, he spreads wings, fans tails, and causes plumage to lift and ripple in the wind, to ruffle, flap, twist, and shimmer, so that his most ambitious carvings simultaneously celebrate the odd beauty of particular species and startle the viewer into a longing for what Robert Penn Warren in his great poem *Audubon: A Vision* calls "a season past all seasons."[7]

"Someone who has known my family
suggested that these herons represented my
two older brothers and me growing up."

The Hammer Galleries exhibition was a great success—but Grainger was burned out. With more money in his pocket than he had ever had at one time, he walked out into a drizzling Manhattan night feeling empty and confused. If this was success, the end toward which he had concentrated his energy and efforts, to the exclusion of family and friends, it left much to be desired. Back on Wadmalaw, he went to work on Adair's farm, driving a tractor until he figured out where to go from there.

A year later, still on the tractor, he invited me for a day of quail hunting. Something had happened since I'd seen him last; he wanted to tell me about it. We drove up to a farm owned by Floride, an hour north of Charleston. It was a good day for following a pair of bird dogs, bright blue and brisk, a good day for sitting on a pine log, talking.

Back in the spring he'd received a call from an old high school friend who was dying of kidney disease and wanted Grainger to come to see him. Grainger wondered what he could possibly say that would make any difference in the face of death, but he went. As it turned out, the friend did the talking. He told Grainger that he had found life in the living Christ, that he was alive now in a way he had never been before.

Grainger had never fretted much about religion. Nominally an Episcopalian, he had dismissed faith as self-deception and managed well enough without it. So he tried to dismiss the light in his friend's eye: a dying man has nothing to lose, he told himself. But that knife cut both ways, and Grainger had to admit that he was in the presence of uncounterfeited peace.

After the funeral Grainger sat alone in his shop. He picked up *The Book of Common Prayer* and read the Apostles' Creed. In spite of his resistance, he knew the time had come to decide one way or the other whether he believed what it said. The moment he realized that,

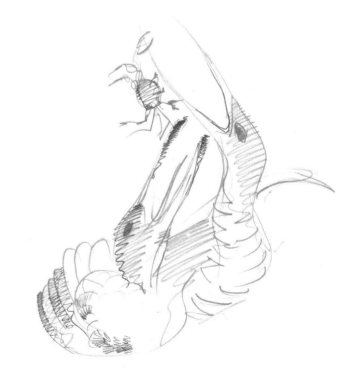

CLAPPER RAILS
1975, Basswood, metal, and oil paint
Collection of Earl F. Slick

he knew that he already had. Months later, sitting on that pine log with me, he still did not fully understand the implications of that decision, but there was no doubt in his mind that he had crossed a continental divide.

Later that afternoon the dogs locked down hard on another covey; we approached, guns up, and the birds flushed in a tight rise, a dozen or more bobwhite quail erupting from our feet. After the shooting and the retrieving, the admiring of the birds and the careful plac-ing of them in our hunting jackets, Grainger said, "Now *that* would be a carving. Maybe the ultimate carving."

A covey rise? I thought. Come on.

A writer's religious faith inevitably affects the way he sees the world. Though he cannot turn his writing into preaching or moralizing and still call it art, he will in all likelihood write about a world ghosted by the supernatural. It makes sense to speak of T. S. Eliot, Flannery O'Connor,

and Walker Percy as Christian writers. But visual art is another matter. As a result of his conversion, Grainger McKoy became a more attentive husband and father and a warmer, more generous friend, but he did not become a better carver. As he said to me, "There's no such thing as a Christian duck." Why then mention his religious life at all? Because in the first place he himself refused to separate it from who he is and what he does, and in the second, the great change that took place in his art, whatever the cause, coincided with his conversion.

Around the time of that hunting trip Grainger and I began a continuing conversation about the possibilities of impressionistic freedom in carv-ing. I already suspected that for me carving was a dead-end street. Whether it was birds as sub-ject matter or carving itself as a medium of aesthetic expression that trou-bled me, I feared that what I found exciting

LEAST BITTERN MODEL

in the watercolors of Winslow Homer and John Singer
Sargent had no counterpart in wooden birds. Grainger,
on the other hand, having mastered the craft and per-
fected the technique of making feathers out of wood,
had grown restless with the prospect of spending the
rest of his life carving birds *trompe l'oeil.* Some new,
unexplored mode surely lay before him, and he was
nosing about for the scent.

On my next trip I saw that he had tacked up by his
work bench photos of Michelangelo's "Captives"—those
massive male figures fighting to free themselves from
stone. They reminded me of what Grainger had said
about carving mallards squirming out of a croker sack,
but he was more interested now in birds escaping from
the wood that contained them. "I could spend the rest
of my life carving the inside of a church," he said. By
way of explanation he showed me photographs of
Grinling Gibbons's carvings for the interior of Saint
Paul's Cathedral: bursting from the walnut dozens of
birds, flowers, and bunches of fruit, the figures unpainted
but identifiable down to plums and plovers. Grainger
said he would like to carve an entire wall of such figures,
to the glory of God, and I realized that he was breaking
free from the safe conventions inherited from both the
decoy and the tradition of bird portraiture.

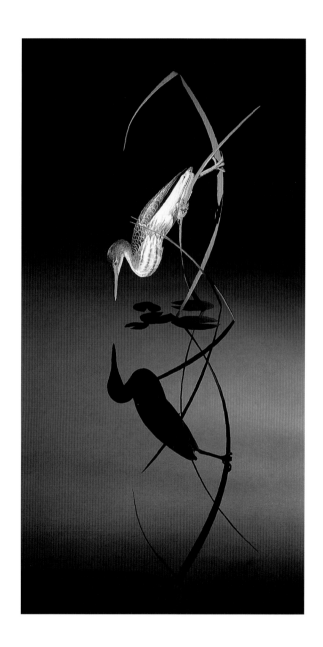

LEAST BITTERN
1987, Basswood, walnut, metal, and oil paint
Collection of Anne D. Wolff

COVEY RISE
(EASTERN BOBWHITE QUAIL)
1981, Basswood, metal, and oil paint
Collection of Earl F. Slick

The break was not clean and sudden. In the summer of '81, on a quick trip to Charleston, I drove out to Wadmalaw. Since my last visit a year before, he had renovated the attic of the country store—painted walls and ceiling white, let in light—and moved his shop upstairs. No longer was he sharing space with Adair's sacks of fertilizer; for the first time he had a real studio. In the center of it stood a work in progress—a carved covey rise. I pulled up a chair; after a while I moved the chair 90 degrees and sat for another spell, and so on until I had circled the sculpture. The ultimate carving, I remembered his having said that day in the field. What I was looking at came close. I counted thirteen quail.

Grainger's genius lies in shaping wood and bending steel to achieve authentic naturalism, but he had never attempted the spontaneous combustion of thirteen flushing bobwhite quail. No one had. The technical difficulty of structuring the design without destroying the natural confusion was daunting. Though I had watched him work on other sculptures, observed his use of Styrofoam mockups, his hollowing out of bodies, and his concealing of steel ribbons, my understanding of technique alone could no more account for what I was looking at than knowledge of sable brushes and transparent pigments can explain a Sargent watercolor.

Pinned up around the work area were sketches of the covey rise, quick pen and inks vibrant with energy: a miniature model of the sculpture sat nearby. A box in a corner was filled with discarded quail—"mistakes," he had decided, though they seemed worthy enough to please many carvers.

The half-finished sculpture stood on a turntable, several individuals still supported by sections of brass tubing clamped to vertical steel rods—a kind of exoskeleton or scaffolding that had allowed Grainger to arrange and rearrange until he achieved the design he sought and then fix it in place by running through it ribbons of steel. I fancied the artist as magician, extending his hand, the artist as God pointing, electric bolts forking from his fingers into and through the positioned birds, hardening into the steel armature that arrested the quail forever in the first half-second of their explosion. That was what I fancied. What I saw was a triumph of engineering, a

"The possibilities for this sculpture sprang into existence on a cold, dreary morning in deep broomsedge. My brother and I, just a few lazy feet apart, instantly and unannounced had quail up our legs."

master feat of balance and cantilever, blueprinted by hard calculation, wrought by drill and torch.

Grainger removed from the back of one of the quail a thin shingle of plumage, a tiny ruffled feather, exposing the joinery of wings to body, steel band to basswood, held together by screws. That steel band extended from the screwed end along the underside of a wing—like the wing's very bone—narrowed and thinned toward its outer end, and emerged from what would become an envelope of feathers as a primary feather itself, indistinguishable from the basswood feathers on either side of it. As hard as that may be to visualize, there was yet another element: that steel primary was connected to the steel primary of an adjacent bird by a tenon and socket joint completely hidden beneath a wing. By such devices had he articulated the sudden flush of thirteen quail.

I reminded Grainger of what he had said that day in the field, about the ultimate carving, and asked how close he thought he had come?

"The ultimate carving would put you in the middle of that covey rise," he said, "birds flying up your pants legs, coming out of your collar, feathers in your face. Now *that* would be the ultimate carving."

From 1978, when he returned to his shop from Adair's tomato farm, until 1983 or '84, Grainger turned out six or seven carvings of individual birds—mostly shorebirds—flushing into flight. *Covey Rise* is the centerpiece of this series, the ultimate burst from concealing cover into the freedom of the air. It also turned out to be the culmination of his conventional decorative period, the masterpiece that leaves you wondering, what's left for him to do?

The answer was suggested by another carving I saw in his shop that day in 1981, a sculpture so quiet and unobtrusive that I almost overlooked it—a dead bird unpainted, half-buried in sand. As astonishing in its own way as *Covey Rise*, the carving was dramatically different from anything Grainger had done before. For one thing, the bird and the sand in which it is buried were carved from a single piece of wood, the exposed half of the bird in bas-relief. The bird—a semipalmated plover—is contrasted to the sand by burned-in plumage, which produces the effect of a pen-and-ink in three dimensions. I was reminded of Michelangelo's "Captives," but whereas those figures are struggling into life, the plover is sinking back into the earth from which it came, one wing lifted by the wind like a defeated flag.

Frankly wooden, *Dead Plover* is an ironic commentary on the artist's previous efforts to bring carved birds to life;

"Walking the beach one fall afternoon, I came upon a spent plover awash with sand. With its last migration behind, it seemed complete when left unpainted."

PLOVER IN SAND
1980, Basswood
Collection of the artist

BLACK SKIMMER
1983, Basswood, walnut, metal, and oil paint
From The Rivers Collection

when compared to the exuberant, ascending liveliness of *Covey Rise*, it gives new meaning to the term "still life."

In preparation for an exhibition at New York's Coe Kerr Gallery in November of 1984, Grainger produced his most frankly impressionistic pieces yet, among them a green-winged teal flushing from an unpainted block of basswood, a Carolina wren emerging from wood, and a mourning dove carved in the form of a taxidermic wall mount. These along with the series of more conventionally conceived birds leaping into flight present a striking contrast to the carvings done before the eighteen-month sabbatical. Whereas those earlier pieces often feature struggle and predation, the later carvings celebrate liberation, the exuberance of taking wing. The pivotal work between these periods was the carving he never made—mallards struggling to get out of a croker sack.

On what turned out to be my last visit to the old Wadmalaw country store, shortly after the Coe Kerr exhibition, I found a new sculpture in the middle of the studio—a black skimmer so boldly conceived that even I was astonished. The skimmer seems to be a favorite subject for carvers, probably because of the bird's large size and dramatic markings, and because its habit of feeding by flying along the surface with its lower beak slicing the water provides a means of support that is rel-

atively easy and strikingly characteristic. Maggioni had carved a skimmer in just that position back in the early '70s, relying on polyurethane to simulate the water. Grainger's bird was "skimming" too, and like Maggioni's earlier one, it was supported at the point where the lower bill makes contact with its reflection in the water, but here there was no water. Taking a risk that no wildlife sculptor had dared, Grainger had mounted the bird upon a three-dimensional image of itself, leaving the water to the viewer's imagination. Not only that, but the "reflection" is sculpted in walnut, not a literal repetition of the subject but an impressionistic correspondence in beautifully lustrous wood.

I stammered my astonishment.

"It didn't sell," Grainger said.

Not long after that visit Grainger and his family moved back to Sumter County, to a place called Stateburg, not far from where he and Floride grew up. I soon abandoned carving for writing, and our paths diverged. As months turned into years, I heard by the grapevine that he was heavily involved in a prison ministry, going behind the walls with other men to share his faith with inmates. Someone told me that he was working on a carving of

"As I was gazing out across a calm, foggy North Edisto,
when the sky and water were one, a black skimmer sliced by,
inspiring me with its reflection."

a flock of sanderlings, and once my father, who lived not far from Sumter County, said he'd heard that Grainger was carving Carolina parakeets.

In the early nineteenth century Stateburg was a thriving town, a contender for the site of the state capital, and home to prominent planters and politicians, among them revolutionary war general Thomas Sumter and Governor Stephen Miller, father of the famous Civil War diarist Mary Boykin Chesnut. Today it is a row of antebellum houses and one Episcopal church, strung out along a ridge that overlooks the Wateree River Swamp, haunted by its history. Governor Miller's house is the one Grainger and Floride bought, a handsome white two-story frame structure surrounded by manicured lawns and flower beds. When I pulled up in front on a clear blue day that autumn, Floride was working in the yard. She pointed the way to Grainger's shop, a small rustic building down on the edge of the woods.

Walking from the house to the shop, I glimpsed the view from the ridge back to the west—in the sloping foreground a pasture and small stable for the McKoys' daughter's horse, off to the right kennels Grainger built for his bird dogs, and beyond, the hazy blue valley of the Wateree River and its vast river-bottom forest, probable site of the great Indian town Cotifichiqui,

despoiled by DeSoto in 1540, and habitat in those days of the ivory-bill woodpeckers and Carolina parakeets.

Grainger came out to greet me, decidedly graying but still trim, still dressed in khaki.

Later that afternoon, on a walking tour of the neighborhood, he told me that his house had been bought sometime in the 1830s by William Ellison, a former slave who because of his skill at building and repairing cotton gins had been able to buy first his freedom, then the Miller plantation, and ultimately sixty-eight slaves, thus becoming the largest black slaveholder in South Carolina. Next door stands the magnificent Borough House, ancestral seat of the locally prominent Anderson family, where botanist Joel Poinsett died. Nearby an odd bit of statuary marks the site of a white oak from which General Sumter hanged two Tory spies. In later days, in an effort to support the historic tree, someone filled its hollow trunk with cement; the sculpture was the "negative" left when the tree rotted away.

It seemed to me, in the deep, green, peaceful shade of his native county, that Grainger had found his true center—a landscape resonant with history, graced with natural beauty, yet shaped and cultivated by him and Floride into a work of art. It was perfect, and I told him I thought so.

"I read a quote of Leonardo da Vinci that
struck a chord in me: 'where the spirit does not
work with the hand there is no art.'"

MOURNING DOVE
1982, Basswood, metal, and oil paint
Collection of Richard P. Mellon

Grainger laughed, said something about its being the right place "for now, for as long as we're here."

What did he mean—that they might move again some day? Or was he talking in terms of time and eternity? Either way, he sounded mighty casual about it.

As he led me into his shop, I wondered what he was working on. I had chosen not to ask, remembering the works in progress I had walked in on before—the *Five Green-winged Teal* on my first trip to Wadmalaw more than fifteen years ago; later, *Covey Rise*, which recreated that covey we had shot the day he told me about the death of his friend; and on my last trip the completed *Black Skimmer*.

And there it was. Before I had had time to survey the shop itself, my eye was drawn to the sculpture in the middle of the room—a flock of Carolina parakeets, five birds—larger than I had expected parakeets to be—tumbling and twisting in wild descent. Toward what? The "habitat" was a simple column of alabaster, the point of support the brush of a wingtip against it.

Maybe it's the Carolina in their name, maybe it's their exotic form and color, or perhaps it's the fact that they have long been extinct, but no other bird when I was a child, not even the ivorybill, so powerfully evoked for me the romantic, moss-hung river swamps of the Carolina low country. My familiarity with the species was limited of course to pictures, particularly to Audubon's, a print of which in double-elephant-folio size, hung on a wall of Grainger's studio. I felt as though I had come to the heart of the old, true South Carolina.

"You know, they roosted in hollow trees," Grainger said.

I did know—but had forgotten.

"Imagine being an Indian, down in the swamp at first light, hunting deer, and that sycamore you're leaning against starts to wake up, comes to life inside, and you look up just in time to see a flock of parakeets swirling out of the top."

This was the second time Grainger had carved parakeets. I asked why.

Something he had read in the *American Ornithology* of Alexander Wilson, he said. When asked about the ability of the parakeet to survive in northern climes, Wilson had claimed to have "seen them, in the month of February, along the banks of the Ohio, in a snow storm, flying about like pigeons, and in full cry."[8]

"I read that and saw the whole carving," Grainger said.

So much for the Carolina low country. Their full cry was obvious. And the alabaster column, I surmised, would somehow become the snow storm, effectively understated.

"These Carolina Parakeets evolved after reading Alexander Wilson's observations in the early 1800s: '…having myself seen them, in the month of February, along the banks of the Ohio, in a snow storm, flying about like pigeons, and in full cry.'"

CAROLINA PARAKEETS
1992, Basswood, metal, and oil paint
Collection of Dan W. Lufkin

Grainger pointed to a bench—his resting place—and suggested I lie down and view the parakeets from that level. He had conceived the sculpture from there, positioned the birds from that angle.

As I lay down, I recognized the music I'd been hearing since entering the room; it was Handel's *Messiah*.

From the bench, the sculpture took on a heightened life. It was as though I had become the target of the flock's descent, a hollow sycamore in which they aimed to roost.

As parakeets inspired what some consider Audubon's greatest painting, so the same bird became the subject of one of Grainger's most impressive sculptures. He completed it in 1992, not long before a retrospective exhibition of his work at the Brandywine River Museum. Located in Chadds Ford, Pennsylvania, home of the Wyeth family, the Brandywine is one of the great conservators of the tradition of realism in American art. To have his work shown there, one floor above rooms that house paintings by N.C. and Andrew Wyeth, was a crowning achievement, a climax commensurate with the level of excellence to which he had brought the art of bird carving.

WOOD DUCK
1984, Basswood, walnut, metal, and oil paint
Collection of the artist

But where would he go from there? After both of
his one-man shows—Hammer Galleries and Coe
Kerr—Grainger had entered upon a period of intro-
spection and reassessment. The husband and father still
had a family to support, children to educate, but the
artist sought new ground. Out of that tension had
come the experiments in impressionism, not all of them
successful. Now with Brandywine behind him, he was
once again anxious to try something different.

Meanwhile, he had two commissions that presented
sufficient challenge to keep him busy. One would be a
sculpture of seven ring-neck ducks coming in, the flock
descending to alight on water supplied by the viewer's
imagination. Grainger had employed that motif several
times before, most notably in *Five Green-winged Teal*, but
in this sculpture the ducks would be attached to a flat
background, a tabby fireplace in a house in Miccosukee,
Florida. The other commission was similar—two
brown pelicans plummeting into the ocean. These birds
also would be attached to a wall, but they would appear
as silhouettes, an effect achieved by the use of unpainted
walnut instead of the usual basswood, and they would
be mirror images of each other.

As Grainger constructed models of the rooms in
which these carvings would be mounted, he found

RING-NECKED DUCKS
1988, Basswood, metal, and oil paint
Collection of Earl F. Slick

himself thinking more and more about an idea that had intrigued him for several years: casting birds in bronze.

When he mentioned that possibility to me, I had trouble taking him seriously. Why, I wondered, would a man who had an almost mystical affinity for wood turn to metal, especially in view of the expense and the technical difficulties of working in the medium? Bronze does not lend itself to the illusion of weightlessness as readily as wood can, nor could I imagine bronze birds rendered in the feathery detail that had from the beginning characterized Grainger's work. What, I asked, was the source of this strange, new impulse?

In the first place, Grainger said, it wasn't new. He had been working with brass and steel from the start, brazing and shaping feet, fashioning support feathers, and designing armatures. Nor was it strange, he said, reminding me of the long tradition of bronze animal sculpture. Indeed, one of his earliest inspirations had been the French bronzes Maggioni had shown him at the Metropolitan Museum.

In order to understand Grainger's success, one has to consider his willingness to take risks that would intimidate many artists. No one, for example, had ever cast a carved bird in the detail that is possible with wood. And that was what Grainger wanted. When he inves-

CAROLINA PARAKEET
1996, Bronze

tigated the possibilities, he was told by every foundry he spoke with that making molds from wood models, especially in a way that would prevent damage to the wood and thus preserve the original, could not be done. Molds were made from clay. Undaunted, Grainger persisted in his search for answers. From a magazine he learned of the process called vacuum casting, by which the creation of a vacuum produces a mold of remarkable resolution. Guessing that the process might work for his purposes, Grainger carved a wren for experimen-tation. Though he had had no instruction in devising a carv-ing from which molds could be made, he followed his intuition, hollowing out the head and breast, shaping wings and coverts that fit together like pieces of a puzzle. When the bird was finished, he videotaped the dismantling and reassembling of its parts, then sent the video along with a letter of inquiry to each of the three foundries that used vacuum casting. The one in Loveland, Colorado, thought they could do it.

Until the wren arrived. Looking at it with the mindset of people who cast from clay, they could not come up with a method of making molds of such delicacy and detail. But fortunately for Grainger, the foundry had an employee with training as a jeweler. His name was Ed Fenton. Ed took the carving home, studied it, and saw a way. When the bronze wren emerged from its cast, Grainger was so pleased that a year later he purchased equipment for a foundry of his own and hired Ed to work it. A few months after that I met Grainger at his farm in Vance. I had never seen him so excited. All he could talk about was bronze birds, the process of casting,

MALLARD HEADS
1998, Bronze

MOURNING DOVES
1997, Bronze

the detail achieved by "pulling a vacuum." He had brought examples, which he displayed on a table. He and Ed had already produced "Wren on Lock," "Carolina Parakeet," "Quail in Hand," and "Woodcock." Ed was making molds for "Barn Swallows" and Grainger was carving "Mourning Doves." He invited me to Stateburg, to meet Ed and see the foundry.

When I arrived, Ed spent an afternoon walking me through the process of casting, from pouring the rubber plug to making blanket molds and mother molds to injecting wax to the final step of pouring molten bronze. The process is far too technical to describe here; the goal, as with any casting, is to create in a hard medium a cavity which is the negative of the model and to fill that cavity with bronze. The difference Ed made was apparent in the fine detail of the molds.

Grainger had finished the carving of the doves. It stood before me in the lustrous umber of burned basswood. Next to it stood a bronze of the same sculpture. The juxtaposition was as close as one might come to seeing wood harden into metal. With no loss of detail. Yet the bronze was something other than a mere metal version of the wood. Somehow it was elemental in a way not true of wood. Then it hit me. The wooden bird, no matter how sophisticated, is and always will be the descendant of the painted decoy, not an inferior medium by any means but one that masks what bronze reveals—an essence of bird that makes color superfluous, a last word.

Audubon said, "in my sleep I continually dream of birds," and Fuertes, in a letter to his old teacher Abbott Handerson Thayer, spoke of the "eye-hunger for these things that get so deeply to you and yours and me."[9] Both artists were bearing witness to a passion for birds, a passion that sustained their art almost literally until the last days of their lives. There are similar testimonials in the writings of George Miksch Sutton, Walter Anderson, and other bird painters. What it amounts to is a fascination so compelling that an artist has to act on it, has to do something about it. Like any passion, it seems strange to those who don't share it, but without it we would have no great bird art. I had wondered for a long time how Grainger might acknowledge that passion in himself. As we were leaving his shop one afternoon, I asked simply, "Why birds?"

The readiness with which he answered indicated a full grasp of the implications of the question. "It started with duck hunting, and that decoy my grandmother gave me. Carving my own helped me come to grips with the

Where two or three are gathered in my name, there am I in the midst of them.
Matthew 18:20

killing." By that he meant that the sadness he felt when he held in his hand the gorgeous drake wood duck he had just shot could be relieved by carving or painting that same bird alive. The labor involved may have been an act of penance, the result certainly a redemption. "My rite of passage," he said, "happened with a duck."

Somewhere in that response lay buried the secret to Grainger's sustained passion. It would be presumptuous of me to attempt to articulate it, but clearly it has to do with the brief lives of birds, with the way in which a bird's fluttering fall portrays our own mortality, and it has to do with the hope we find in the freedom of their flight, the impulse to immortality they so beautifully suggest.

I once asked Grainger what he planned to carve next. He laughed. "Maybe what I'll carve next is my tombstone. Carve it out of locust wood. Ray Beddingfield, that old friend of mine from up in the mountains, told me once that a locust post would wear out *two* holes. That ought to make a good tombstone. I want to hang it in that doorway, so every time I go in and out I'll be reminded of what really matters."

James Kilgo is a professor of English at the University of Georgia in Athens. He is the author of two essay collections, Deep Enough for Ivorybills *and* Inheritance of Horses, *and a novel,* Daughter of My People.

NOTES

1 Mary Ann Livingston and Nora E. Taylor, "'Incredibly Lifelike' Animal Models in Wood," *Christian Science Monitor*, April 11, 1974, F-5.

2 Roger Schroeder, "From Sticks to Steel: A Short History of Birds in Flight," *Wildfowl Carving and Collecting* 5, no. 2 (Summer 1989): 26.

3 Mary Terry, "Soaring Art: Grainger McKoy Overcomes Static Elements to Capture Motion in Wood Sculpture," *The State* (Columbia, S.C.), July 20, 1975, F-1.

4 Margaret Nichols, *Bird Sculpture: A Native American Art Form, Refined*, exh. cat. (Birmingham, Ala.: Birmingham Museum of Art, 1976).

5 Vladimir Nabokov, quoted by Adam Gopnik, "Audubon's Passion," *The New Yorker* 67, no. 1 (February 25, 1991):96.

6 Gopnik, "Audubon's Passion," p. 96.

7 Robert Penn Warren, *Audubon: A Vision* (New York: Random House, 1969), p. 29.

8 Alexander Wilson, *American Ornithology* (London: Ballantyne, n.d.), 1:378.

9 Audubon as quoted in Warren, *Audubon*, p. 26; Fuertes to Thayer, April 1916, as quoted in Robert McCracken Peck, *A Celebration of Birds: The Life and Art of Louis Agassiz Fuertes* (New York: Walker, 1982), p. 94.

BARN SWALLOWS
1997, Bronze

Wood Process

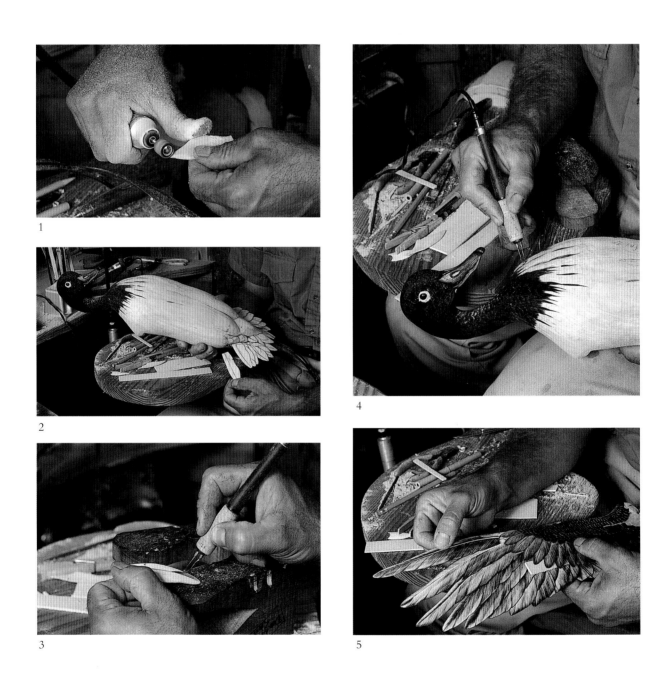

Grainger begins by cutting out feather forms from a piece of basswood. Then, he smoothes them with a sanding wheel (1). He then draws "barb" lines and checks their positioning (2). Next, he burns in feather patterns with a hot etching pen (3,4) and then sets them in place to form a wing or a tail of a bird (5).

Bronze Process

Rubber molds are made from wood originals. Wax is then injected into the molds forming a wax piece identical to the wood original (1). Ceramic molds are then created, the wax is burned away and bronze is poured in its place (2). After removing the bronze pieces from the mold they are arranged (3) and welded together to complete the sculpture (4). Finally, an oxidizing agent is applied by hand to achieve the patina (5).

Catalogue of the Exhibition

Selected Bibliography

Badger, Curtis. "Grainger McKoy: The Journey through Life and Art." *Wildfowl Art* (Winter 1990-91): 29-32, 54-55.

Bailey, Jim. "The Real McKoy." *Charleston* 5, no. 1 (January-February 1991): 32-35.

Basile, Kenneth. "Grainger McKoy." *Ward Foundation News* 9, no. 1 (Winter 1985): 2-5.

_____. Introduction to *Grainger McKoy: Recent Work*. Exhibition catalogue. New York: Coe Kerr Gallery, 1984.

Birmingham Museum of Art. *Bird Sculpture: A Native American Art Form, Refined*. Exhibition catalogue. Birmingham, Alabama: by the museum, 1976.

Brakefield, Tom. "Wood Takes Wing." *Sports Afield* 181, no. 1 (January 1979): 56.

Brandywine River Museum. *Bird Sculpture in Wood by Grainger McKoy*. Exhibition catalogue. Chadds Ford, Pennsylvania: by the museum, 1993.

Bryant, Nelson. "Wood, Field, & Stream: The Art of Bird Carving." *New York Times*, March 22, 1974.

Buerschaper, P., and David Lank. *Animals in Art*. Exhibition catalogue. Toronto: Royal Ontario Museum, 1983.

Carter, Art. *The Sporting Craftsmen*. New Albany, Ohio: Countrysport Press, 1994: 202-203.

Dickey, Gary. "Woodcarving Revolution." *South Carolina Wildlife* (November-December 1975): 9-15.

Hammer, Victor. Introduction to *Grainger McKoy: Woodcarved Wildlife Sculpture*. Exhibition catalogue. New York: Hammer Galleries, 1976.

Hoving, Thomas. "My Eye: Diogenes-Come-Lately." *Connoisseur* (February 1985): 15.

Kilgo, James. "Sixteen Sculptures: The Birds of Grainger McKoy." *Georgia Review* (Spring 1993): 61-64.

Leigh Yawkey Woodson Museum. *Birds in Art*. Exhibition catalogue. Wausau, Wisconsin: by the museum, 1998.

Livingston, Mary Ann, and Nora E. Taylor. "'Incredibly lifelike' animal models in wood." *Christian Science Monitor*, April 11, 1974.

Nichols, Margaret. "Birds in the Wood." *Field & Stream* 79, no. 5 (September 1974): 45-46, 136.

Nutt, Amy. "Art on the Wing." *Sports Illustrated* 79, no. 24 (December 13, 1993).

Pridgen, Margaret. "When Wooden Birds Take Wing." *Clemson World* 43, no. 3 (Fall 1990): 12-17.

Robertson, Pat. "The Oyster House Connection." *Sporting Classics* 2, no. 4 (September-October 1983): 35-45.

Schroeder, Roger. "Birds in Flight: The Carvers' Techniques." *Wildfowl Carving and Collecting* 5, no. 2 (Summer 1989): 25-30.

_____. "Grainger McKoy's Carved Birds." *Fine Wood Working* 32 (January-February 1982): 77-80.

Sozanski, Edward. "The real McKoy: An exhibition of carved birds." *The Philadelphia Inquirer Magazine*, July 23, 1993.

Warrington, Charles E. "Expression takes Flight: Works of Grainger McKoy." *Wildfowl Carving and Collecting* 5, no. 2 (Summer 1989): 53-57.

Wechsler, Charles. "Art & Etc." *Sporting Classics* 17, No. 6 (November-December 1998): 40, 43, 45.

Wolff, Theodore F. "The Craft Comeback: The Many Masks of Modern Art." *Christian Science Monitor*, November 29, 1984: 46.

This catalog has been published in conjunction with an exhibition of
Grainger McKoy's sculpture at:
Brookgreen Gardens
Pawley's Island, South Carolina
March 13–December 31, 1999.

Published by Wyrick & Company
1-A Pinckney Street
Charleston, SC 29401

Designed by Gil Shuler Graphic Design, Inc.
Printed in Hong Kong

Library of Congress Cataloging-in-Publication Data

McKoy, Grainger
The sculpture of Grainger McKoy / introduction by Robin R. Salmon;
essay by James Kilgo.
p.   cm.
Published in conjunction with an exhibition held at Brookgreen
Gardens, Pawley's Island, S.C., Mar. 13-Dec. 31. 1999.
Includes bibliographical references (p. 64).
ISBN 0-941711-44-7 (pbk.)
1. McKoy, Grainger—Exhibitions. I. Kilgo, James. 1941-   .
II. Brookgreen Gardens. III. Title.
NB237.M375A4   1999
730' 93—dc21   98-49880
CIP

Most of James Kilgo's essay, "The Art of Grainger McKoy," was previously
published in the catalog *Bird Sculpture in Wood by Grainger McKoy* for an
exhibition held at the Brandywine River Museum, Chadds Ford,
Pennsylvania, June 5–September 6, 1993, and is reprinted with the permis-
sion of the Museum and the author.

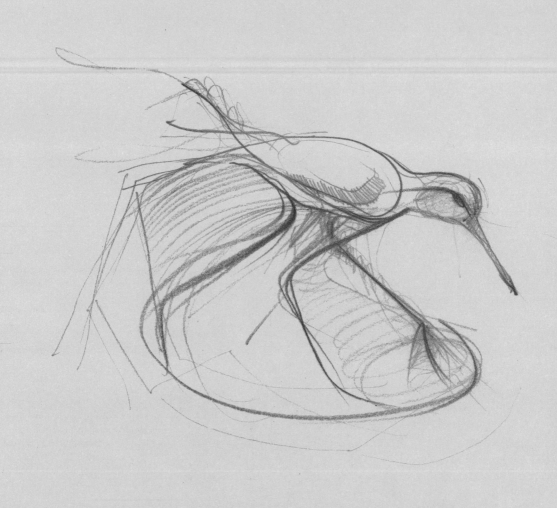